EVEN MORE! ELEMENTARY WRITING PROMPTS

FOR RELUCTANT WRITERS

OVER **40** MORE PROMPTS!

MICHAEL FISHER
WITH **LILY AND CHARLOTTE FISHER**

Even More Elementary Writing Prompts for Reluctant Writers
©2020 by Michael Fisher
A Digigogy.com Publication

Special Thanks to Christina Quinn, teacher at North Tonawanda Middle School in North Tonawanda, NY for her #1 HITS contribution.

Published by:
The Digigogy Collaborative
Amherst, NY
WWW.DIGIGOGY.COM

Cover Design by Michael Fisher
Interior Design by Michael, Lily, and Charlotte Fisher
Editing by Michael, Lily, and Charlotte Fisher

ISBN: 9798669531386

First Printing: July, 2020

WE HAD SO MUCH FUN CREATING A BRAND NEW BOOK OF WRITING PROMPTS! LIKE THE LAST BOOK, THIS BOOK OF PROMPTS IS ABOUT ALL KINDS OF WRITING. IT IS NOT NECESSARILY BASED ON THE DEVELOPMENT OF ANY PARTICULAR SKILL BEYOND JUST IDEA GENERATION AND PUTTING WORDS TO PAPER. IT IS AN OPPORTUNITY FOR WRITERS TO WORK FROM WHEREVER THEY ARE, ENJOY THE ACT OF CREATING SOMETHING, AND TO HAVE FUN WITH WORDS.

WE HOPE YOU ENJOY BEING CREATIVE! WE DID!

-MICHAEL, LILY, & CHARLOTTE FISHER

ANIMAL WHISPERS

YOU JUST DISCOVERED THAT YOU CAN TALK TO AN ANIMAL. JUST ONE ANIMAL AND NOT ANY OTHERS. WHICH ANIMAL CAN YOU TALK TO AND WHAT WOULD YOUR CONVERSATION BE? DRAW A PICTURE OF YOUR ANIMAL AND THEN WRITE OUT YOUR CONVERSATION. USE THE BOXES BELOW TO WRITE OUT WHAT YOU SAY AND WHAT THE ANIMAL SAYS IN RESPONSE!

DRAW IT!

WRITE IT!

MORE SPACE...

YOU FLY INTO A PORTAL THAT TAKES YOU TO ANOTHER DIMENSION! WHAT HAPPENS WHEN YOU FLY THROUGH THE PORTAL?

ANOTHER DIMENSION!

MORE SPACE...

A TEXTING CONVERSATION BETWEEN YOU AND THE ARTIFICIALLY INTELLIGENT ROBOT YOU CREATED.

ARTIFICIAL INTELLIGENCE

MORE SPACE...

ON YOUR NEXT BIRTHDAY, ONE OF YOUR GIFTS IS TO BE BIGGER OR SMALLER. YOU GET TO CHOOSE. WRITE ABOUT WHAT WILL HAPPEN IF YOU WERE BIGGER OR SMALLER.

BIGGER OR SMALLER?

_____

_____

_____

_____

_____

_____

_____

_____

_____

_____

MORE SPACE...

BOOK ADVISOR

☆ ☆ ☆ ☆ ☆

HOW MANY STARS DO YOU GIVE YOUR BOOK?

DRAW YOUR BOOK COVER

TITLE: _____

_____

_____

_____

DESCRIBE YOUR BOOK

BOOK REVIEW:

WRITE ABOUT WHAT YOU LIKED OR DIDN'T LIKE. WHAT MIGHT YOU TELL THE AUTHOR?

MORE SPACE...

_____

_____

_____

_____

_____

_____

_____

_____

_____

_____

_____

_____

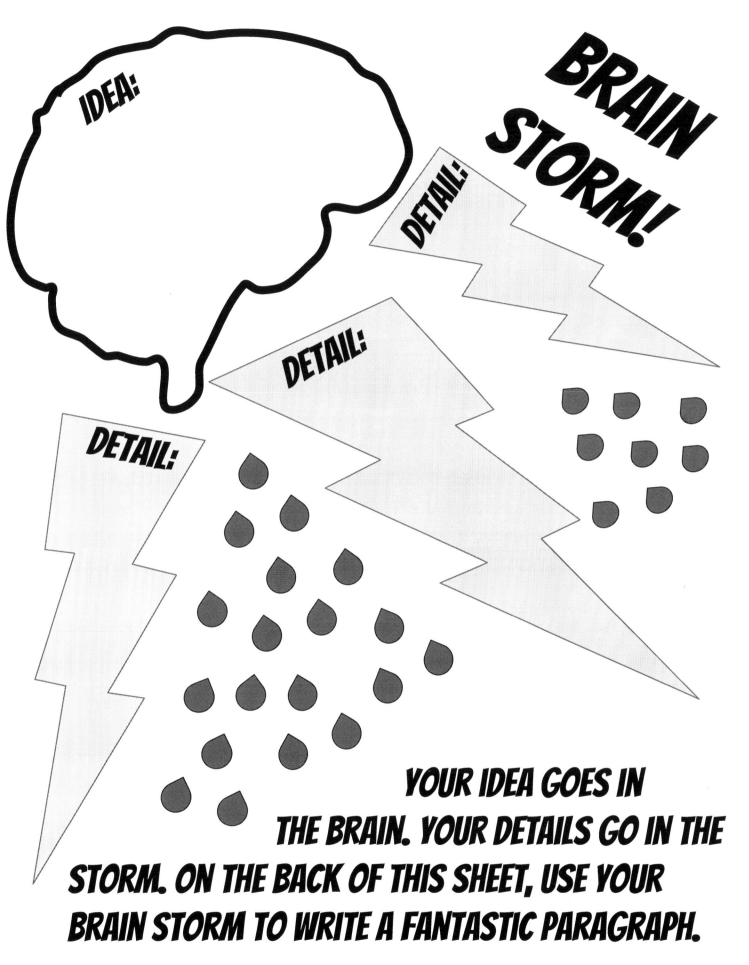

©2020 www.digigogy.com

MORE SPACE...

THE OAK AND THE REEDS

A Giant Oak stood near a brook in which grew some slender Reeds. When the wind blew, the great Oak stood proudly upright with its hundred arms uplifted to the sky. But the Reeds bowed low in the wind and sang a sad and mournful song.

"You have reason to complain," said the Oak. "The slightest breeze that ruffles the surface of the water makes you bow your heads, while I, the mighty Oak, stand upright and firm before the howling tempest."

"Do not worry about us," replied the Reeds. "The winds do not harm us. We bow before them and so we do not break. You, in all your pride and strength, have so far resisted their blows. But the end is coming."

As the Reeds spoke a great hurricane rushed out of the north. The Oak stood proudly and fought against the storm, while the yielding Reeds bowed low. The wind redoubled in fury, and all at once the great tree fell, torn up by the roots, and lay among the pitying Reeds.

Better to yield when it is folly to resist, than to resist stubbornly and be destroyed.

BRANCHING POEMS

BRANCHING POEMS ARE CREATED BY SELECTING AND CIRCLING INDIVIDUAL WORDS IN A LARGER TEXT. DRAW LINES TO CONNECT THOSE CIRCLED WORDS TO THE BRANCHES OF THIS TREE. YOUR POEM IS MADE UP OF THE WORDS YOU CIRCLED. READ IN ORDER FROM TOP TO BOTTOM.

NOTE: YOU COULD USE YOUR OWN TEXT ON ANOTHER SHEET OF PAPER AND DRAW YOUR OWN TREE...

MORE SPACE...

CLAY-CRAFT!

DRAW IT!

GRAB SOME CLAY OR BENDY PIPE CLEANERS AND CREATE SOMETHING COOL. DRAW A PICTURE OF YOUR CREATION ABOVE AND THEN DESCRIBE IT BELOW!

DESCRIBE IT!

MORE SPACE...

CRAZY RECIPES!

CRAZY RECIPES HAVE RIDICULOUS AND GROSS INGREDIENTS. THEY GET MADE IN THE WEIRDEST WAYS AND WHEN THEY ARE DONE, THEY LOOK DELICIOUSLY AWFUL! WHAT CAN YOU COME UP WITH?

INGREDIENTS:

PROCEDURE:

DRAW THE FINAL PRODUCT:

MORE SPACE...

DESCRIBE, THEN COLOR, THE CRAYONS BELOW. CREATE NEW COLOR COMBINATIONS AND THEN NAME THEM SOMETHING REALLY FAR OUT!

CREATIVE CRAYON COLORS!

NAME:
DESCRIPTION:

NAME:
DESCRIPTION:

NAME:
DESCRIPTION:

NAME:
DESCRIPTION:

NAME:
DESCRIPTION:

NAME:
DESCRIPTION:

NAME:
DESCRIPTION:

NAME:
DESCRIPTION:

MORE SPACE...

CUTE TO CREEPY!

PICK AN ANIMAL, A FAVORITE STUFFED TOY, OR DOLL AND DRAW A PICTURE OF IT IN THE CUTE BOX. ON THE LINES BELOW, WRITE WORDS THAT DESCRIBE YOUR CUTE DRAWING. THEN IN THE CREEPY BOX, REIMAGINE YOUR DRAWING AS CREEPY, WRITING CREEPY DESCRIPTIVE WORDS BELOW IT!

CUTE!

DRAW IT!

CREEPY!

DRAW IT!

DESCRIBE IT!

DESCRIBE IT!

MORE SPACE...

DELETE / REPLACE

DELETE ONE THING IN YOUR FIELD OF VIEW AND REPLACE IT WITH SOMETHING RIDICULOUS. FOR INSTANCE, I MIGHT DELETE THE TREE IN MY FRONT YARD AND REPLACE IT WITH A GIANT UNICORN-THEMED WATER SLIDE. I MIGHT CHANGE MY COFFEE CUP INTO A CHINCHILLA OR MY SOFA INTO A GIANT BANANA SPLIT. BE CREATIVE ABOUT WHAT YOU MIGHT DELETE AND REPLACE THEN WRITE ABOUT HOW THAT REPLACEMENT WILL IMPROVE OR DISRUPT YOUR

DELETE:	REPLACE:

_____

_____

_____

_____

_____

_____

_____

MORE SPACE...

DESCRIPTIVE WORDS

THINK OF A NOUN (A PERSON, PLACE, OR THING). WRITE IT IN THE MIDDLE BELOW. IN THE SPACES AROUND THE MIDDLE, WRITE AS MANY ADJECTIVES (DESCRIPTIVE WORDS) YOU CAN THINK OF. AT THE BOTTOM WRITE A SHORT PARAGRAPH USING YOUR NOUN AND ALL OF YOUR DESCRIPTIVE WORDS.

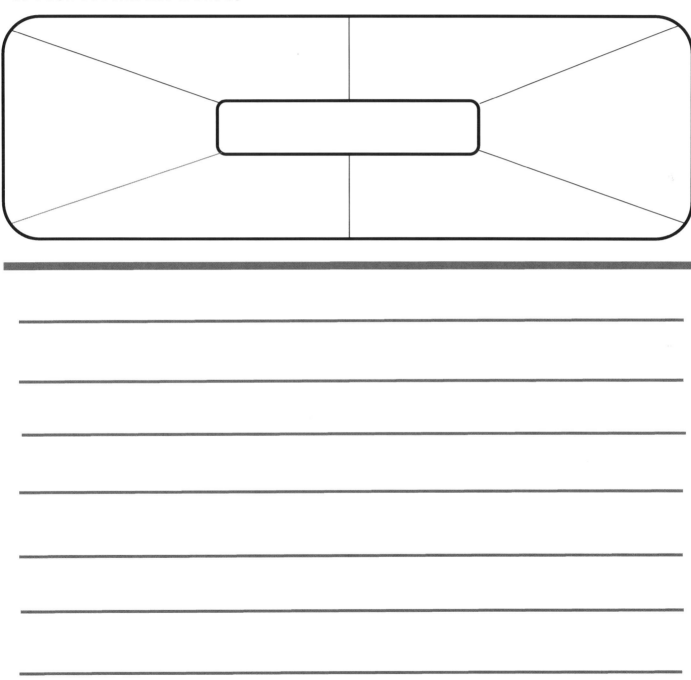

MORE SPACE...

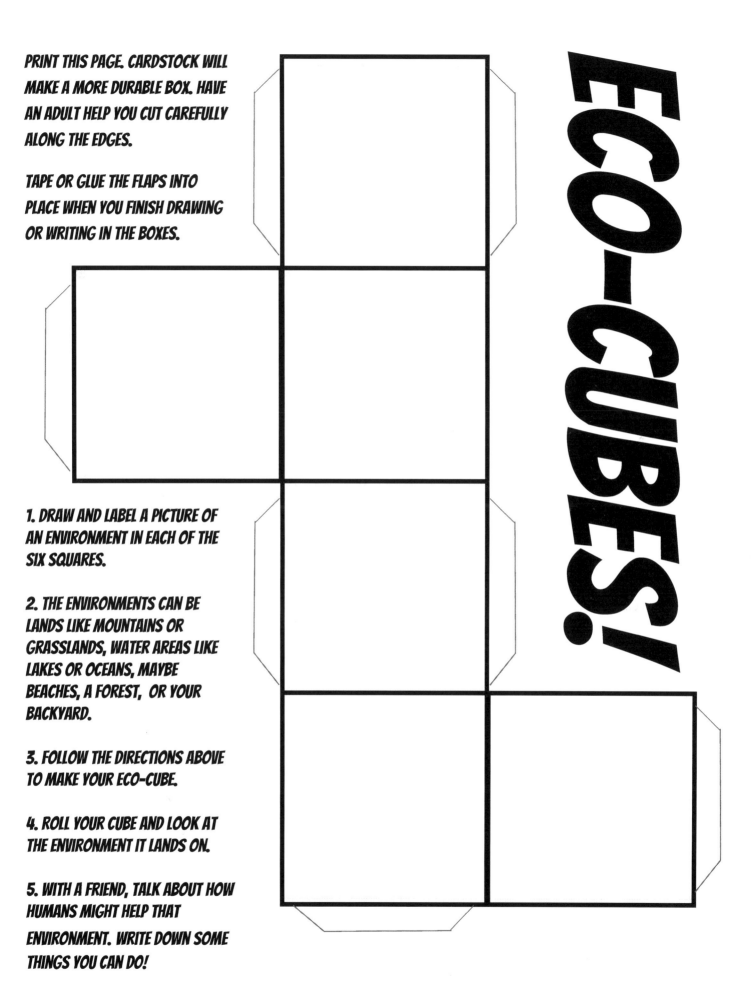

PRINT THIS PAGE. CARDSTOCK WILL MAKE A MORE DURABLE BOX. HAVE AN ADULT HELP YOU CUT CAREFULLY ALONG THE EDGES.

TAPE OR GLUE THE FLAPS INTO PLACE WHEN YOU FINISH DRAWING OR WRITING IN THE BOXES.

ECO-CUBES!

1. DRAW AND LABEL A PICTURE OF AN ENVIRONMENT IN EACH OF THE SIX SQUARES.

2. THE ENVIRONMENTS CAN BE LANDS LIKE MOUNTAINS OR GRASSLANDS, WATER AREAS LIKE LAKES OR OCEANS, MAYBE BEACHES, A FOREST, OR YOUR BACKYARD.

3. FOLLOW THE DIRECTIONS ABOVE TO MAKE YOUR ECO-CUBE.

4. ROLL YOUR CUBE AND LOOK AT THE ENVIRONMENT IT LANDS ON.

5. WITH A FRIEND, TALK ABOUT HOW HUMANS MIGHT HELP THAT ENVIRONMENT. WRITE DOWN SOME THINGS YOU CAN DO!

MORE SPACE...

EMOJI COMMOTION!

WRITE A SENTENCE BELOW ONLY USING EMOJIS. THEN DRAW A PICTURE IN THE BOX THAT GIVES A CLUE ABOUT YOUR EMOJI SENTENCE. WRITE THE TRANSLATION OF YOUR EMOJI SENTENCE AT THE BOTTOM. FOLD THE TRANSLATION ON THE DOTTED LINE AND FIND A FRIEND TO SHARE WITH. SEE IF THEY CAN FIGURE OUT YOUR EMOJI SENTENCE!!

EMOJI SENTENCE:

_____

_____

_____

TRANSLATION:

_____

_____

_____

MORE SPACE...

FASHION DESIGNER!

T-SHIRTS OFTEN HAVE WITTY PHRASES OR POPULAR SAYINGS ON THEM. WHAT CLEVER SLOGANS OR CATCH PHRASES CAN YOU COME UP WITH? WRITE THEM ON THE SHIRTS BELOW AND THEN DECORATE TO COMPLETE YOUR FASHION STATEMENTS!

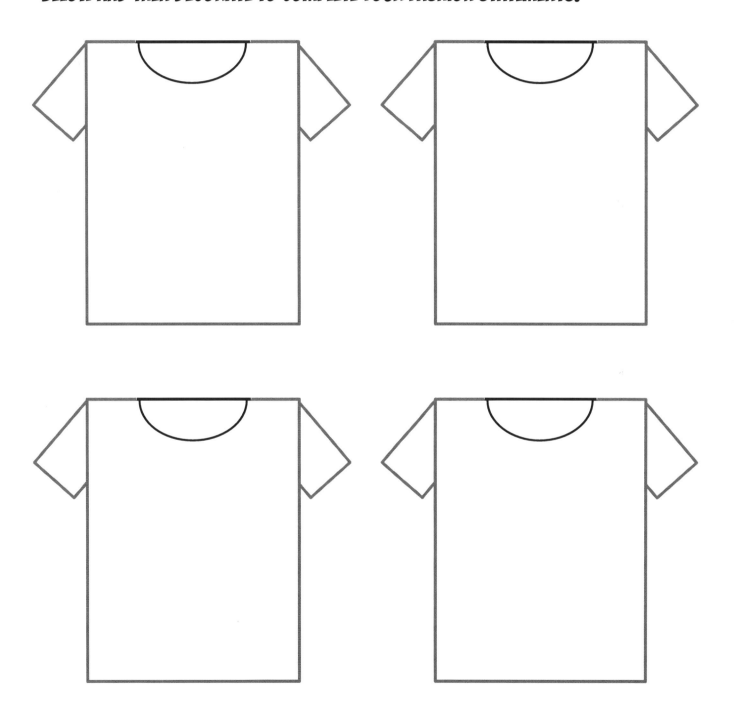

MORE SPACE...

GHOST AGENT!

YOU'RE A REAL ESTATE AGENT BUT FOR GHOSTS. YOU HELP THEM FIND PLACES TO HAUNT. YOU JUST FOUND A NEW HOUSE FOR YOUR GHOSTLY CLIENTS BUT THEY ABSOLUTELY MUST NEVER GO IN THERE. WHY?

_____

_____

_____

_____

_____

_____

_____

_____

MORE SPACE...

KEYBOARD CLACKS!

IF YOU'VE EVER JOKINGLY CLICK-CLACKED ON A KEYBOARD, YOU KNOW THAT YOU GET A RANDOM BUNCH OF LETTERS THAT MIGHT LOOK LIKE THIS: LSKFGNSOFGNP. FOR THIS PROMPT, DO A QUICK CLICKAROUND / RANDOM TYPING ON A KEYBOARD OR JUST PICK A FEW RANDOM LETTERS. RECORD THE LETTERS IN THE BOXES BELOW, THEN WRITE A SENTENCE WHERE EACH WORD BEGINS WITH THOSE LETTERS IN ORDER! SEE HOW CREATIVE YOU CAN BE!

MORE SPACE...

LOOK UP AT THE STARS!

GO OUTSIDE WHEN IT IS DARK AND LOOK UP AT THE SKY. FIND A CONSTELLATION AND DRAW A SKETCH OF IT. AN HOUR OR TWO LATER, GO BACK OUTSIDE AND WRITE A SENTENCE ABOUT WHAT HAPPENED TO THE POSITION OF YOUR CONSTELLATION.

TIME YOU WENT OUTSIDE THE FIRST TIME:

_____

TIME YOU WENT OUTSIDE THE SECOND TIME:

_____

DRAW YOUR CONSTELLATION.
DO YOU KNOW YOUR CONSTELLATION'S NAME? _____

WHAT HAPPENED TO THE POSITION OF YOUR CONSTELLATION THE SECOND TIME YOU WENT OUT?

_____

_____

MORE SPACE...

MAGIC BOOGERS!

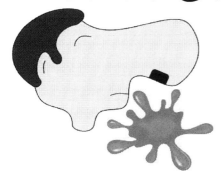

YOU DISCOVER THAT YOU HAVE MAGIC BOOGERS. WHAT IS THEIR POWER AND HOW DO YOU USE THIS POWER?

WHAT'S YOUR BOOGER POWER?

_____
_____

HOW DO YOU USE THIS BOOGER POWER?

_____

_____

_____

_____

_____

_____

MORE SPACE...

MAKE YOUR OWN COMIC!

USE THE DOTTED LINES TO SEPARATE THE MAIN BOXES INTO HALVES OR FOURTHS!

THIS WORD BUBBLE IS FOR WHEN CHARACTERS SPEAK.

THIS WORD BUBBLE IS FOR WHEN CHARACTERS THINK..

THIS BOX IS FOR EXPLANATIONS: CHARACTERS, SETTINGS, ETC.

MORE SPACE...

MEME-ORIES!

REMEMBER THAT TIME YOU PICKED YOUR NOSE AT THE ZOO?

YEAH, HE REMEMBERS TOO.

DRAW OR PASTE PICTURES IN THE BOXES THAT REPRESENT MOMENTS YOU REMEMBER. USE THE WHITE AREAS TO ADD YOUR TEXT TO MAKE YOUR OWN MEME-ORIES. CUT THEM OUT AND SNEAK THEM INTO FAMILY PHOTO ALBUMS, FRAMED PICTURES AROUND YOUR HOUSE, OR MAYBE STICK THEM IN SOMEONE'S PACKED LUNCH!

MORE SPACE...

_____

_____

_____

_____

_____

_____

_____

_____

_____

_____

_____

_____

MESSAGE IN A BOTTLE!

YOU FIND A MESSAGE IN A BOTTLE! WHAT DOES IT SAY? WHAT IS YOUR RESPONSE? MAKE THIS EVEN MORE FUN BY ASKING A FRIEND OR FAMILY MEMBER TO WRITE THE MESSAGE IN THE BOTTLE. THEN, YOU RESPOND TO IT!

THE MESSAGE:

_____

_____

_____

_____

THE RESPONSE:

_____

_____

_____

_____

MORE SPACE...

_____

_____

_____

_____

_____

_____

_____

_____

_____

_____

_____

MONSTER APPLICATION!

YOU WANT TO BE A MONSTER IN A KID'S CLOSET BUT YOU HAVE TO APPLY! FILL OUT THIS APPLICATION TO SEE IF THE NITE-TIME MONSTER COMPANY WILL HIRE YOU! JUST FOR FUN, SHARE THE COMPLETED APPLICATION WITH A YOUNGER BROTHER, SISTER, OR COUSIN!

REAL NAME:

MONSTER NAME:

SHARE YOUR FAVORITE WAYS TO SCARE OTHERS:

WHAT SCARY THINGS HAVE YOU DONE IN THE PAST?

WHAT SCARY THINGS WOULD YOU LIKE TO TRY IN THE FUTURE?

USE THIS SPACE AND THE BACK OF THIS PAGE TO WRITE ABOUT A TIME WHEN YOU REALLY SCARED SOMEONE ELSE!

MORE SPACE...

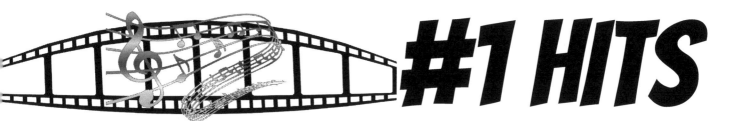

#1 HITS

ASK AN ADULT IN YOUR FAMILY ABOUT THEIR FAVORITE SONG WHEN THEY WERE YOUR AGE. FIND THEIR SONG ON YOUTUBE OR SPOTIFY OR ANOTHER MUSIC SERVICE AND LISTEN TO IT OR WATCH THE MUSIC VIDEO. WRITE YOUR FAMILY MEMBER'S SONG IN THE BLANK BELOW AND DESCRIBE WHAT YOU LIKE AND DON'T LIKE ABOUT THEIR SONG. WRITE DOWN YOUR FAVORITE SONG AND LET YOUR FAMILY MEMBER LISTEN TO IT. HAVE THEM WRITE DOWN WHAT THEY LIKE AND DON'T LIKE ABOUT YOUR SONG!

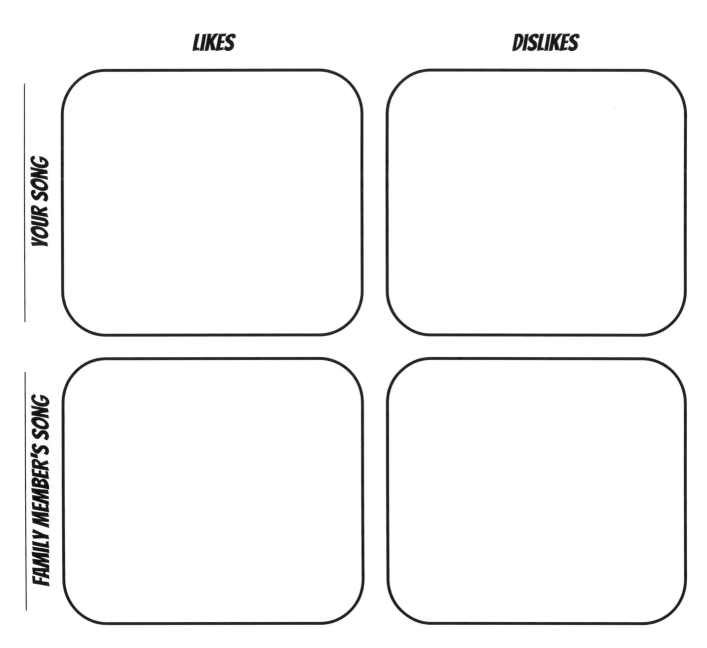

MORE SPACE...

PLANT A SEED AND GROW YOUR OWN FRUIT, VEGETABLE, OR HOUSEPLANT! MAKE A LIST OF MATERIALS YOU MIGHT NEED TO GET STARTED. THINK OF WHETHER YOU WANT TO PLANT YOUR SEED OUTSIDE OR INSIDE. THEN, THINK OF HOW YOU WILL TAKE CARE OF YOUR PLANT WHILE IT SPROUTS AND AS IT GROWS!

LIST OF MATERIALS:

HOW YOU WILL CARE FOR IT:

PLANT A SEED!

MORE SPACE...

PORTMANTEAU!

A PORTMANTEAU IS A GRAMMATICAL DEVICE THAT BLENDS PARTS OF TWO WORDS TO FORM A WORD THAT IS SIMILAR IN MEANING TO THE WORDS THAT WERE BLENDED. SEE SOME EXAMPLES BELOW AND THEN MAKE YOUR OWN CREATIVE COMBINATIONS! (CREATINATIONS? COMBREATIVES?)

WORD ONE:	PORTMANTEAU:	WORD TWO:
BREAKFAST	BRUNCH	LUNCH
GIGANTIC	GINORMOUS	ENORMOUS

MORE SPACE...

_____

_____

_____

_____

_____

_____

_____

_____

_____

_____

_____

POSITIVE PEBBLES!

WRITE AND DECORATE POSITIVE MESSAGES ON THE PEBBLES BELOW. YOU COULD DESIGN YOUR PEBBLES HERE, THEN DECORATE REAL PEBBLES TO HIDE AROUND YOUR NEIGHBORHOOD!

MORE SPACE...

_____

_____

_____

_____

_____

_____

_____

_____

_____

_____

_____

_____

WHAT CAN YOU USE LESS OF?

_____

_____

_____

_____

WHAT CAN YOU USE AGAIN?

_____

_____

_____

WHAT CAN YOU RECYCLE?

_____

_____

_____

_____

_____

_____

_____

_____

_____

_____

_____

_____

REDUCE.
REUSE.
RECYCLE.

MORE SPACE...

ROLL A STORY!

ROLL A DICE FOR EACH OF THE COLUMNS. WHATEVER NUMBER YOUR DICE LANDS ON, CHOOSE THAT WORD OR PHRASE. ROLL FOUR TIMES TO FIND OUT WHO, WHAT, WHERE, AND WHEN. WRITE YOUR STORY USING THOSE FOUR ELEMENTS ON THE BACK OF THIS PAGE! SHARE YOUR STORY WITH A FRIEND!

	WHO?	WHAT?	WHERE?	WHEN?
1	BABY	FINDS SOMETHING	IN A DARK CAVE	WHEN DINOSAURS LIVED
2	WEREWOLF	HEARS SOMETHING	ON ANOTHER PLANET	DURING A THUNDER STORM
3	SCUBA DIVER	BREAKS SOMETHING	AT THE GROCERY STORE	ON THE HOTTEST DAY OF SUMMER
4	YOUNGER SIBLING	HIDES SOMETHING	AT THE BEACH	IN THE MIDDLE OF THE NIGHT
5	ACTOR / ACTRESS	EATS SOMETHING	AT A SPORTS EVENT	DURING A PARADE
6	ASTRONAUT	FEELS SOMETHING	AT A CAMP	AFTER A BIG MEAL

MORE SPACE...

SPIRAL POEMS!

ON THE BACK OF THIS PAGE, WRITE 3-4 SENTENCES ABOUT SOMETHING YOU REALLY ENJOY: A GAME, A HOBBY, A SPORT, A CRAFT, ANYTHING! THEN COME BACK TO THIS SIDE AND WRITE YOUR SENTENCES ONE RIGHT AFTER THE OTHER ON THE LINE BEGINNING IN THE MIDDLE OF THE SPIRAL! TURN THE PAGE AS YOU WRITE TO STAY ON THE LINE. THAT'S HOW YOU MAKE A SPIRAL POEM!

MORE SPACE...

SPY-KU IS A HAIKU THAT YOU WRITE ABOUT SECRETS YOU SPY. A HAIKU IS A THREE-LINED POEM WHERE THE FIRST LINE HAS FIVE SYLLABLES, THE SECOND LINE HAS SEVEN SYLLABLES, AND THE THIRD LINE HAS FIVE SYLLABLES. THESE POEMS DON'T RHYME. WHAT DO YOU SPY WITH YOUR LITTLE EYES? WRITE YOUR SPY-KU BELOW!

_____ (5)

_____ (7)

_____ (5)

_____ (5)

_____ (7)

_____ (5)

_____ (5)

_____ (7)

_____ (5)

MORE SPACE...

STICK-Y NOTES!

YOU'VE HEARD OF STICKY NOTES, RIGHT? HOW ABOUT NOTES ON ACTUAL STICKS? WRITE YOUR NOTES ON THESE STICKS, CUT ON THE DOTTED LINES, AND STICK YOUR STICK-Y NOTES ANYWHERE!

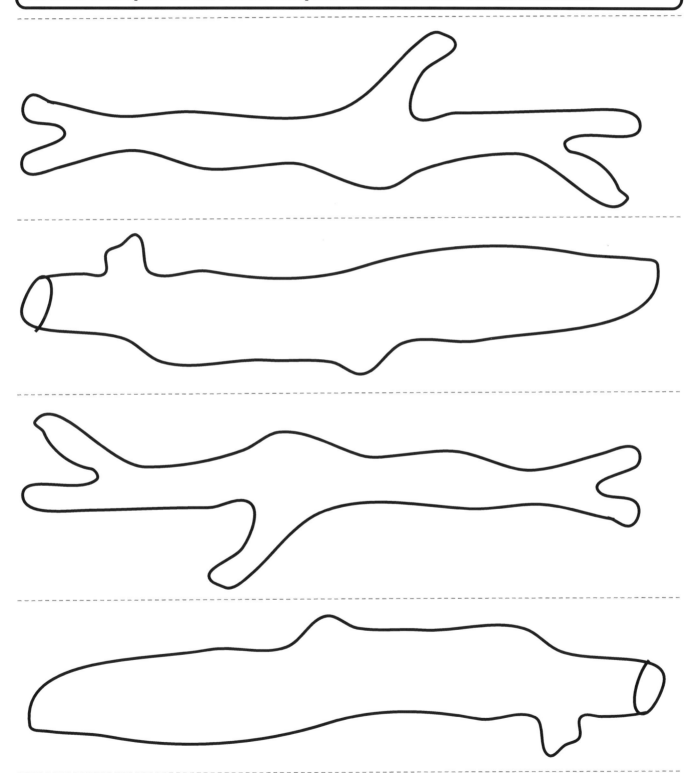

MORE SPACE...

SURVIVAL!

FIND A PLANT AND AN ANIMAL. DRAW A PICTURE OF EACH. THEN, MAKE A LIST OF THINGS THE PLANT AND ANIMAL NEED TO SURVIVE. WHAT'S THE SAME? WHAT'S DIFFERENT? DO OTHER PLANTS AND ANIMALS NEED THE SAME THINGS? WHAT DO YOU NEED TO SURVIVE?

DRAW YOUR PLANT

DRAW YOUR ANIMAL

PLANT NEEDS:

ANIMAL NEEDS:

MORE SPACE...

_____

_____

_____

_____

_____

_____

_____

_____

_____

_____

_____

SURVIVAL MODE!

YOU WAKE UP IN MINECRAFT SURVIVAL MODE. YOU CAN ONLY HAVE FIVE TOOLS. WHAT ARE THEY AND HOW WILL YOU SURVIVE THE NIGHT?

_____

_____

_____

_____

_____

_____

_____

_____

MORE SPACE...

TALENT SHOW!

YOU'RE THE DIRECTOR OF A TALENT SHOW STARRING YOUR FAMILY AND FRIENDS. IN THE SPACES, WRITE DOWN WHAT THEY MIGHT PERFORM AND WHAT THEY WILL WEAR. THEN JUDGE THEIR PRETEND PERFORMANCE! BONUS POINTS IF YOU CAN ACTUALLY GET THEM TO DO IT!

PERFORMER NAME:

PERFORMANCE:

COSTUME:

JUDGING:

PERFORMER NAME:

PERFORMANCE:

COSTUME:

JUDGING:

PERFORMER NAME:

PERFORMANCE:

COSTUME:

JUDGING:

PERFORMER NAME:

PERFORMANCE:

COSTUME:

JUDGING:

PERFORMER NAME:

PERFORMANCE:

COSTUME:

JUDGING:

MORE SPACE...

THE NEXT GREAT PERFORMER

DRAW A PICTURE OF A PERFORMER. THEN DESCRIBE THE PERFORMANCE. THE PERFORMANCE CAN BE REALLY GOOD OR REALLY AWFUL. PRETEND YOU'RE A JUDGE. DOES THE PERFORMER GO TO THE NEXT LEVEL OR NOT?

DRAW IT!

DESCRIBE IT!

MORE SPACE...

_____

_____

_____

_____

_____

_____

_____

_____

_____

_____

_____

_____

YOU'VE BEEN BITTEN BY A THWUMPAFLUFFLE. EVERYONE REACTS DIFFERENTLY TO THEIR BITES. HOW DO YOU REACT?

_____

_____

_____

_____

_____

_____

_____

_____

THWUMPAFLUFFLE

MORE SPACE...

_____

_____

_____

_____

_____

_____

_____

_____

_____

_____

_____

_____

TWEET THE GIST!

FOR THIS TASK, YOU'RE GOING TO CREATE BRIEF GIST STATEMENTS ABOUT TEXTS YOU'VE READ AND THEN "POST" THEM TO TWITTER. THE GIST OF A STORY, BOOK, OR ARTICLE IS LIKE A BRIEF SUMMARY OF WHAT THE TEXT IS ABOUT. ON TWITTER, YOU ONLY HAVE A FEW CHARACTERS TO SHARE YOUR MESSAGE AND THE SAME IS TRUE HERE. FEEL FREE TO USE CHARACTERS LIKE " & " FOR "AND," OR THE NUMERIC "1" INSTEAD OF "ONE" TO KEEP YOUR TWEETS SHORT AND SIMPLE! USE THE TWEET BOXES BELOW TO TWEET THE GIST ABOUT ONE TEXT OR MULTIPLE TEXTS!

@THEGIST

_____

_____

03:05 PM - May 8, 2020 from Anytown, USA

@THEGIST

_____

_____

03:11 PM - May 8, 2020 from Anytown, USA

@THEGIST

_____

_____

03:18 PM - May 8, 2020 from Anytown, USA

MORE SPACE...

UPLOAD!

WHAT IF YOU COULD UPLOAD YOURSELF TO THE INTERNET AND GO VISIT ALL THE COOL WEBSITES OR GAMES YOU LIKE? INSTEAD OF STARING AT A SCREEN, YOU COULD BE IN THE WEBSITE OR GAME! MAKE A LIST OF YOUR FAVORITE WEBSITES OR GAMES IN THE BOX TO THE RIGHT. THEN PICK ONE TO WRITE ABOUT WHAT WOULD HAPPEN IF YOU WENT FOR A VISIT!

FAVORITE WEBSITES OR GAMES:

WHAT HAPPENS WHEN YOU GO INSIDE?

MORE SPACE...

WHEN IT IS COLD, WHAT IF IT SNOWED FROZEN PEAS OR ICE CREAM SANDWICHES? WHAT IF RAIN WAS GINGER ALE OR CHICKEN BROTH? WHAT IF THE WIND CAUSED TORNADOS OF TOMATOES? WHAT IF YOU WERE THE WEATHER FORECASTER THAT HAD TO TELL YOUR AUDIENCE ABOUT THE WACKY WEATHER? WRITE YOUR WACKY WEATHER FORECAST BELOW! IF YOU WANT TO GET REALLY CREATIVE, RECORD YOURSELF IF FRONT OF A MAP OR GREEN SCREEN AND READ YOUR FORECAST ON A VIDEO TO SHARE!

WACKY WEATHER FORECASTS

MORE SPACE...

WAYS YOU HAVE BEEN HONEST

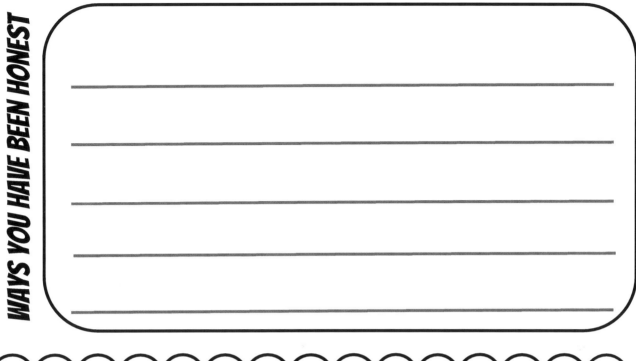

WE CAN ALWAYS BE HONEST!

WRITE ABOUT WAYS YOU HAVE BEEN HONEST AND WAYS YOU COULD BE HONEST IN THE FUTURE!

WAYS YOU COULD BE HONEST

MORE SPACE...

_____

_____

_____

_____

_____

_____

_____

_____

_____

_____

_____

ZOO CLUES!

USE AWESOME ADJECTIVES TO DESCRIBE AN ANIMAL AT THE ZOO! WRITE OUT YOUR DESCRIPTIVE WORDS IN THE BOXES THEN HAVE A FAMILY MEMBER OR FRIEND TRY TO FIGURE OUT YOUR ANIMAL ON THE LINES BELOW!

WHAT ANIMAL AM I?

WHAT ANIMAL AM I?

WHAT ANIMAL AM I?

WHAT ANIMAL AM I?

MORE SPACE...

MICHAEL, LILY, &
CHARLOTTE FISHER

LIST OF FIGURES AND ATTRIBUTION.

All images are either public domain, Creative Commons including commercial usage with attribution, or freely available to use with all sources cited below.

Made in the USA
Middletown, DE
09 August 2020